TABLE OF CONTENTS

From Tragedy to Triumph

RON WISE

DEDICATION

I dedicate this book to my beloved father Mr. Randy M. Wise.

FORWARD

I have had the pleasure of knowing Mr. Ron Wise since 2013. We immediately had a mutual respect for one another. By the time we first met, Mr. Wise had been well adjusted to his spinal cord injury and the difficulty with day to day functioning. However, he was always looking for ways to improve his function. For all the time I've known him, he has always been a strong advocate for his care and very knowledgeable with his condition. Whether it be online support groups or scientific research studies, he always brings the latest information and questions to clinic visits. As his rehabilitation physician, it is rewarding to see a patient who actively participates in his care.

What makes Mr. Wise a remarkable human being is not his tenacity and his determination to overcome his disability and functioning at his highest potential, but his dedication to helping others and the community. He is a very committed father, husband, role model, and mentor to his family, patients with spinal cord injuries, and the community at large. His impact far outreaches his presence, as evidenced by the establishment of Wise Choice Ministries.

I am thrilled to have the honor to share with you a few words about Mr. Wise. This book is a wonderful narrative of Mr. Wise's life, filled with images of a hard-working man, who overcomes an unfortunate injury that left him with a long-lasting disability. Despite his devastating injury, he continues to lead a life of positivity and Godly manner, a sure example of a wonderful human being and a role model to others. I hope you enjoy reading through Mr.

Ron Wise

Wise's journey as I continue to marvel at his accomplishments.

Kenneth Ngo, MD

INTRODUCTION

I was born and raised on the south side of Chicago in the early 70`s. The south side was a middle-class neighborhood, most often with two parents working or one parent working multiple jobs. In my household, I had a sister who is two years older than me, a mom and dad who both worked outside the home. My sister and I attended catholic schools from elementary to high school. Residing in a middle-class neighborhood, our neighbors respected one another and kept us out of trouble. With this support we didn't have problems with authority figures or the law. After high school my sister attended college and I immediately started working along-side my dad in a part time summer position at a refinery corporation. My dad has always worked hard and provided the family with everything we needed and most of what we wanted. He became my role-model and a great person to mirror. I really admired his hard work ethics and giving me a great example of what man-hood should look like. My mom was a strong woman who also worked very diligently to help support the family financially and made sure we had the nurturing that was needed. She molded the first example of what a mother and wife should reflect. She was always classy and ladylike. She also made sure we had hot meals to eat, clothes on our backs and made the house a home. My parents worked hard together to instill moral values in us that served us well into adulthood.

Attending Catholic schools most of my life, we rarely attended church; not because we didn't believe in God, but it was not a priority at that particular time. I learned, as most kids did, that God was real and also how to pray but He remained a distant mystery to me. I was taught the meaning of prayer, but I only used it to get something I wanted. I continued to have this callous relationship with God until my mid-twenties.

I met Shana at a job seminar where we became friends and soon after started dating. She was from Kalamazoo, Michigan visiting her dad in Chicago. Since she was not from Chicago, I used to show her around the city and take her downtown to the Sears Tower observatory deck to have dinner and talk about life and our future. We also enjoyed other restaurants and just being in each other's presence. After dating for several months, we fell in love and she got pregnant and moved back to Kalamazoo, where she had more support from her mother, brother and other family members. At the time I was working a full-time construction job in the suburbs of Illinois. It paid well and overtime opportunities were readily available which I took advantage of. I would work 12 to 14 hours every day, and on Fridays I would get off work and drive about three hours to Kalamazoo to see Shana for the weekend. Then I would drive from her house back to work. My visits never seemed long enough. We would always discuss one of us relocating. Both of us wanted to move out of our hometown, so we discussed moving to Indiana. After I applied to several jobs in Indiana and looked at several housing opportunities, we both decided to just settle down in Kalamazoo.

It was very difficult for me to move from a city I had known, to a city I knew very little or nothing about. I was reluctant because of my fear of the unknown. I worried about my relationship with her and what the future held for us. I had family, including two young boys by different women. I had to consider the impact it would have on their lives and our relationship. Me, Shana and boys would go to the beach, park and various other places. We all had a good time together and the boys enjoyed being around her. I could see the love she had for them and the love they had for her. Those times were very influential, as she would encourage me with positive thinking and a different outlook on life. All of those things I had to take in consideration as I contemplated moving. I would not be available to pick them up and drop them off at school or be available at a moment notice if they needed me. That caused me great concern. It was very important to me that my three and four years old boys bonded together at a young age as they had different mothers and that would not happen if I was unavailable.

I really didn't want to leave them behind and I was having thoughts of uncertainty. I began to ask the Lord to give me a sign if he wanted me to move to Michigan. (I don't know what made me call on the Lord for assistant….it wasn't like I knew Him like that, but I had heard others talk about how God will answer prayers. But I wasn't even thinking about that, I needed to decide and I just wanted a sign to help me). It seemed a little strange at the time, but I would see several license plates that were from Michigan. I disregarded it and said, "that's just a coincidence". Then I would ask the Lord again, "Lord if you want me to move to Michigan please give me another sign". Then I would see a Michigan commercial that would invite viewers to Michigan. At that time the Lord had my attention, but I still was not positive that was Him speaking to me. Then

3

one day while I was on lunch break at a restaurant, a coworker and I were sitting in a booth. Right behind me was a couple of guys engaged in a conversation. One of the guy's daughter was moving from Chicago to attend college in Michigan! Wow! That's when I thought it was really God, so I decided to move. I was sure that moving to Michigan was the Lord's will.

Within the next few days I was excited and sad at the same time. I was unsure how my boys were going to react and what their relationship would be without them interacting with each other on a daily basis. One Saturday, I picked up my boys for an evening at the park. We talked about my moving away and coming back to visit them in Chicago and them coming to see me on the weekends in Michigan. They were upset and confused. They didn't know if they would see each other or me on a regular basis. But after I assured them I would only be two hours away, they were a little more accepting.

Even though I knew this move was God's will, it was still a very difficult decision. Nevertheless, with all jitters, nervousness and uncertainties that I had, I was obedient to the Lord and packed up and moved

I concluded that this was God's way of communicating with us. Sometimes we expect miraculous events or look for something grand…but He simply put me in the right places at the right time. This really starting me thinking more about this God that I had heard so much about. I wanted to know more about Him and how He works in ordinary people lives.

Shortly after moving to Kalamazoo, Shana got pregnant

again. We were already facing trying times as we were combining lives and struggling with figuring out life. I was working a full-time construction job which had me traveling all over the state. I would work out of town all week then return home on Friday evenings. This job was very lucrative but it still posed a problem of me being absent from the home for a week at a time. I was paying just over $800 a month in child support for my two boys in Chicago and Shana was at home with a two-year-old and pregnant. We would often argue about me traveling out of town all week with my job and her being at home with no emotional or moral support from me. I applied for different jobs in town and shortly afterwards landed a local construction job. I enjoyed working this job because it allowed me to be home every night with Shana and she enjoyed it as well. It didn't pay as well, but the trade-off for me being at home every night was well worth it. We got married in 2001 in a small church one Sunday morning after church service. It was a small wedding with a few family members and some of our closest friends. Needless to say, I was nervous and second-guessing myself. I was concerned about the success of the marriage and all other uncertainties. Not only was I concerned about my thoughts, I was also concerned about her thoughts as well. I could only imagine what her thoughts were, and if they were anything like mine, we were in trouble. But I soon realized that was normal to feel that way and concentrated on a positive outcome instead of the negativity. After the wedding we had a small reception at my mother-in-law house and started our life as a married couple. Our finances were challenged and that put a strain on our marriage. I now had three kids with one on the way and I was unsure about the decisions that I had made to relocate to Kalamazoo. It was an easy decision to move back to Chicago and pick up where I left off, but we were determined to remain together despite the odds being against us.

I continued to work long hours throughout the week and the weekends to make ends meet. Shana would attend church regularly and would encourage me to go with her. At the time I was working long hours to make up the difference with the child support I was paying. Those hours did not allow me to attend church regularly. She would tell me what she learned in church and how much she enjoyed it. After a while of hearing how much she enjoyed attending church, I was curious and made sacrifices to start attending with her.

I enjoyed church and soon became a member with Shana. Soon afterwards, my fourth kid was born (Justin) and I was excited and nervous, because I had yet another mouth to feed. Shana went back to work as a medical assistant and soon decided to further her education. She became a nurse which lightened the financial burden for us. I felt a lot of pressure to be successful not only with my marriage, but as a good father. I really enjoyed attending church, as it was very influential in our life. That's when I began to learn and experience the true nature of God.

Writing this book is a therapeutic endeavor for me. It affords me an opportunity to share my testimony in the hopes it will help someone who is facing some monumental difficulties. I want to let them know that God is always there to comfort and give you peace. You must trust him and continually work your faith as you'll see in the following chapters. Secondly, this book is my personal offer of praise, honor and glory that I give to my Lord and Savior Jesus Christ. I am delighted that you chose to take this journey with me as I re-live one of the most difficult times of my life. It's my desire that you will be encouraged to keep moving forward and be blessed.

Ron Wise

CHAPTER 1
MAKE NO ASSUMPTIONS

I woke up on October 29, 2011 about 5:45am and hurriedly got dressed. My job started at 6:30 am. I had been late a couple of times that week and my boss had counseled me on being punctual and ready for work. When I got up I had to rush to get in the shower, brush my teeth and find something to wear for the day. I kissed my wife goodbye and we wished each other a good day. I ran down the stairs, grabbed my keys and jumped into the car. I backed out the driveway and traveled my daily route to work. There were at least two alternate routes that I could have taken, but for some reason I had chosen this particular route. It was a route that I was familiar with, but rushing to get to work, I disregarded some of the precautions, like the speed limit, weather, visibility, and other increased traffic. I needed to get to work on time and everything else became secondary to me. I went to grab the steering wheel with both hands and realized I had a second set of keys in my hand. I had mistakenly grabbed my wife's keys along with mine. She would not be able to go to work, so I had to return home to drop off her keys.

Now, I'm on my way back to work. Trying not to be late, I was going at a high rate of speed. I usually have my seatbelt buckled, but on this day, it seemed less important. As I was approaching a deep curve in the road, I believed I could maintain my speed and still manipulate the curve. I soon learned I was very wrong in my assumption. At that time, I was not thinking about my safety or other motorist, I was only thinking about arriving to work on time. The sun had not yet come up, so it was still dark out, and the traffic was very minimal. As I approached the curve, I attempted to drive through it. I slowed down to navigate the curve but it was too late. The car began to veer off the road, as the road was a little damp from the morning dew. In an attempt to regain control, I overcorrected the car and it began to flip over and over and over, for a total of three times. I can recall thinking, "what have I done"? I had not been in a car wreck in over 20 years and everything was happening so fast that it was mentally difficult for me to keep up with what was transpiring at that moment. After flipping a total of three times, the car then came to rest in a ditch right-side up. As I lay in the center of the console, I was thinking, "I'm definitely not going to make it to work on time or even make it to work at all"! I tried to sit up-right to climb out of the car. I was unable to move my torso or my legs to accomplish what other-wise would've been a simple task. I wasn't in any pain so I couldn't figure out why I was unable to move my body. I slowly examined myself to see if I had any broken bones. As I lay there, I heard another motorist driving by. I wasn't sure what was going on with my body and I wasn't sure if this was going to be my final resting place or would I be rescued?

Now I'm getting a little worried. Even though I still didn't feel any pain, I thought seriously that this might be my last day. I began to think about my family and how life was going to be without me. I strangely felt calm and at peace with everything that had taken place up to this point. I was willing to accept my fate without complaining. The sun had not come up yet, which caused another sense of concern. The car I was driving was dark green and it was lying in a deep ditch full of green vegetation camouflaging the car. That was going to make it more difficult for someone to find me!

During that time, I remained calm, knowing that there was only one thing I was in control of... My faith! I began to call out to the Lord, not asking for anything, but thanking him for everything that he had done for me and my family. Generally, no one would be thanking God at this particular time, but I didn't want to complain on what might be my last day here on earth.

In my mid 20's I had given my life to Christ. People need to understand that being a Christian does not mean you are perfect. You will continue to make mistakes and fall short. But what it does mean is that there is someone who is faithful and willing to forgive you! I have not been perfect throughout my life and I have repented for several things I've done. I didn't want to die without acknowledging how good God had been to me and my family. I wanted to give him the praise and glory he deserved, as if those were my last breaths. I also thought about my family… my parents, my kids, my wife and my sister. How and what they would do? My mind went into overdrive and started to brainstorm all sorts of things.

The car was completely smashed, except for one headlight that was still illuminated towards the street. I know the Lord allowed that one light to stay intact, as it was a beacon light shining out of the ditch. It allowed a motorist to see it and get me the help I so desperately needed. As I lay there, I heard a car stop and a door close. Then I heard a voice yell "are you okay"? In a faint voice I said, "No, please get some help". A few minutes later I heard sirens. I've heard emergency vehicle sirens before, but this time it was different. This time when I heard them, they were coming to respond to me. As they got closer, the sirens became louder and everything became surreal. Surprisingly I was still calm up to that point. As the paramedics approached the car, I became nervous and frighten. The paramedics immediately started asking me a series of questions. What is your name? Where do you live? Where do you work? All these questions were an attempt to keep me coherent. When the firemen arrived, he briefed me on what they were about to do. They told me because the doors were all crushed downward they were unable to remove me from the doors or the windows, so they were going to cut the roof off to remove me from the car. I said, "Do whatever you have to do to get me out of here". After they removed the roof from the car, they put a brace around my neck, lifted me up and placed me on a gurney. As they carried me up the ditch, I can recall the roads being blocked off and traffic being redirected. As they carried me into the ambulance, I asked one of the paramedics," What type of injury do I have?" They said they were not sure, but the doctor would let me know after he sees the x-rays".

Ironically, my wife and I had purchased a vehicle two months prior, changed insurance companies and upgraded our policy to a full coverage premium (no-fault) package. The insurance coverage before the upgrade was limited liability which would not have covered any hospital visits, surgeries, medication etc. In addition, the previous few years I had worked an abundance of overtime which had allowed my family to live comfortably. In retrospect, I realized that God had allowed the overtime to be readily available and allowed me to be healthy enough to work 16-hour shifts days on end for several years because he knew my destiny. God is always in control and does what's best for us even if we fail to accept it or realize it." For your father knows the things you have need of before you ask him" (Matt.6:8).

The normal commute to the hospital takes about seven minutes, but this seemed like an eternity. When I arrived at the E.R., medical staff was awaiting me at the door. They rushed me back to a room to prepare me for surgery. The nursing staff asked me was there anybody I would like to call. I said," yes, my wife". The nurse took my phone and scrolled through the call log and called my wife. I heard the nurse tell her I was in a terrible car wreck and she needed to get to the hospital as soon as possible. They did not give her any details about my condition. A few minutes later she arrived and was very distraught. I was very concerned as I scrambled for the right words to say in an attempt to calm her down. I knew I had to be stronger than what I looked like. I began to reassure her and calm her down as best as I could. I later learned that one of the vehicles that were rerouted from the car wreck was hers. She had no idea they were detouring her because her husband was lying near dead in a ditch!

Trained as a nurse, Shana knew the prognosis of many patients in my condition. She had seen patients walk again and she had seen patients that were totally dependent upon a caregiver. I could not feel my body or move it in any kind of way. I began to talk to her, but they were not my words…. I told her that I will walk again and be the man she needed me to be. I had no idea what was going on with my body or what the outcome was going to be. I certainly didn't have any idea whether I would be able to walk again or be the man she needed me to be! But the Holy Spirit began to speak to her through me. I know it was the Holy Spirit, for I could not say the words I was saying to her on my own.

The Holy Spirit is what God left us with when Jesus died upon the cross." Greater is he that is within me than he who is in the world" (1 John 4:4). I thank God for the Holy Spirit, because it truly is a comforter in a time where everything seems to be in disarray. I remember trying to calm her down and telling her everything was going to be okay. She was crying and very upset. As a prayer warrior, she knew nothing else to do but pray and have people at my side praying for me and with me, so she called my mom in Chicago and our Pastor Addis Moore of Mt. Zion Baptist Church.

Shortly after pastor Dr. Moore and Deacon Van Burch were the first to arrive at the hospital. There were other pastors, deacons, ministers, and a swarm of other saints there and they were praying for me. As I thought about how everything had transpired, I thank God for preparing me for such a day as this. As I mentioned, over the past few years God had prepared my wife and I by equipping us with his Word. "In the beginning was the Word and the Word was with God and the Word was God" (John 1:1).

We are forever thankful that we attended a Bible teaching ministry under the leadership of our pastor, Dr. Addis Moore. He taught us the power of prayer, having faith in God and a host of other biblical teachings. If we had not been under his leadership, we would not have been able to handle this. We had learned a lot under his preaching, teaching and leadership. We had learned how to apply biblical teaching and application throughout our life. I thanked my pastor for his obedience, guidance and Christian education, because through him Jesus saved my life and allowed me to testify about how good God is.

I sometimes feel unworthy of all the blessings He has bestowed upon me and my family. I had been disobedient in so many areas of my life, but I repented for my sins and asked for forgiveness. Even though I have repented for my sins and ask for forgiveness, the devil continued to taunt me with my transgressions.

The devil would have me to think that I didn't deserve to live, and it was my fault for rushing and not wearing a seatbelt, I was not going to regain a reasonable portion of my body strength, and capabilities. This is the kind of thinking that leads to depression and stagnate your mental and physical healing. I knew the devil was still out to get me, so I had to fight back with the word of God. "The thief comes to kill still and destroy. I came that they may have life, and that they might have it more abundantly" (John 10:10). As I laid there trying to pull myself together from the devils hold, my wife came back into the room with a modest smile on her face. I felt relieved that she could still look at me and smile. At that point I knew she would be okay. She later told me that my room was overflowing with family and friends. As a result, the medical staff had to escort them to a waiting room where there was standing room only. Words can't express how much that meant to me. I did not realize how many people cared about me. They were at my bedside and overflowing in the waiting room. They were all on one accord praying for me and the well-being of my family. I recall my pastor and a couple of deacons at my bedside holding my hands and praying for and with me. God allowed me to stay coherent to tell my story and testify in detail how good God is and what he can do through the power of prayer and worship. I thank God for all saints who were at the hospital praying for me and the ones who were unable to make it were praying on my behalf.

The doctor performed a sensory test on my body which consisted of asking me a series of questions. I recall the doctor asking me if I could move my toes and or feet, I replied no. He asked me if I could move my legs or feel his touch, I replied no. He asked me if I could move my hands or arms, I replied no. He then asked me if I could move my head, and once again I replied no. They then rushed me back for x-rays and I awaited the results, the doctor returned to the room, and told me I had a broken neck and I had sustained a spinal cord injury and they had to perform emergency surgery. At that time, I was given medication and rushed into surgery.

After surgery, all of my family was in the recovery room. Then I was placed in the intensive care unit. While in ICU I had a very difficult time dealing with my physical capabilities. I assumed that after surgery I would be able to utilize my body like I did prior to the car wreck, but I was greatly disappointed. I had a neck brace on and I was still unable to move. I started to get upset and depression slowly started to set in. I thought about the remainder of my life, being paralyzed and bed-ridden. I tried very hard to be and think positive thoughts, but what I was seeing and going through made it very difficult to be positive at all. That day that I had the car wreck played over and over again in my mind. I couldn't help but think about if I had not been in such a rush and driving so fast, none of this would have happened. I was upset with what I had done to myself and my family and I found it difficult to forgive myself. I thought about what life will be like if I never walked again, played basketball or football with my sons, or even take my daughter to the father-daughter dance. I also thought about not being able to take my wife out for a night on the town. I thought about what my life would be like and the quality thereof. None of this was making sense to me. What was the point of having surgery if I still felt the same and was still unable to move? I had so many questions and concerns. Needless to say, I was very afraid and uncertain of what my future held, but it didn't look good at all. I was always the protector of my family and now I felt like all my guards were down and I was very vulnerable. I asked the Lord to not only heal me, but make me whole again. I wanted to return to the life as I knew it. I knew how to provide and strive for my family, but this new life was strange, scary and very foreign to me and I wanted no part of it. I had a difficult time trying to understand what was going on with my body. The next few days I asked a lot of questions while trying to cope with this new person I had become. Dr. Joshua Ellwitz of Bronson Methodist Hospital performed my surgery and informed me that I would need a lot of therapy and I would be transferred to a rehabilitation hospital.

After five days of intensive care, I was transferred to Mary Free Bed Rehabilitation Hospital in Grand Rapids, Michigan.

FROM TRAGEDY TO TRIUMPH

CHAPTER 2
REHABILITATION

When I arrived at Mary Free Bed, I had a reality check! I realized that I was a totally different person than I was prior to the car wreck. I was in a lot of pain, taking a lot of medication and starting to come out of the lethargic state of mind that I had been in for the last five days. I still didn't understand what was going on with my body and/or how to use it for normal activity.

The first night was really rough for me. It was difficult to sleep, or just to be comfortable in bed. I was very agitated because I didn't know what to think about my condition, my future or anything else. I had never taken medication before in my life and now I was taking a fistful of medications- in the morning, noon and night. I remember lying in bed asking for pain medication. My neck was in excruciating pain! I had never felt this kind of pain before in my life.

The next day Dr. Ho entered my room to educate me about the kind of injury I had sustained. He informed me that I had suffered an incomplete spinal cord injury and I was going to need a lot of rehab, moral and spiritual support. Your spinal cord is a bundle of nerves that runs down the middle of your back. It carries signals back and forth between your body and your brain. A spinal cord injury disrupts the signals. Spinal cord injuries usually begin with a blow that fractures or dislocates your vertebrae. Most injuries don't cut through the spinal cord. Instead, they cause damage when pieces of the vertebrae tear into the cord tissue or press down on the nerve that carry signals. Spinal cord injuries can be complete or incomplete. With a complete SCI, the cord can't send signals below the level of injury. As a result, you are paralyzed below the injury. Incomplete SCI you have some movement and sensation below the injury but bodily functions are greatly diminished and chances of walking

18

were close to none. He went on to say I had broken vertebrae C3-C6 in my neck. Those vertebrae were fused with two plates and eight screws. I asked him, "When will I be able to walk again and use my body the way I used to?" He answered me and said, "That all depends on how hard you work in therapy". That wasn't the answer I wanted to hear. I wanted him to tell me that in a few days I'd be discharged and back to work on light duty for a couple of weeks then full duty after that. But I was a long way off with my assumption. Little did I know, life for me would never be the same.

I enjoyed watching TV in bed, but now I was unable to turn the channel with the remote control, so one of the technicians adapted a mechanism to the control called a sip and puff. This device was clamped to the hand rail of the bed with a long tube that came from it to my mouth. It was controlled by air going into it or air coming out of it. I had to sip it to change the channel on the TV and had to puff it to call the nurse. This took a little getting used to, because if I sipped it one too many times and passed a program I wanted to watch I had to sip several times to get back to the program. This was just one of many adaptations that I would be making in the months to come.

My mom and two oldest sons arrived from Chicago. They were looking sad and worried. It was very uncomfortable for them to see me like this, but they tried to be strong and not let me see them worry, but I saw right through them. They didn't know what to say or ask, so they just looked and tried to make small talk. It was at that point the Lord had given me motivation that fueled me to fight for what the enemy thought he had stolen. We are merely flesh and blood traveling through this thing we call life, as if we're on a highway trying to get to our final destination which is our heavenly home. If you allow him, he will turn your mess into a message and your test into a testimony! My mom was by my bedside rubbing my legs, arms and hands, asking if I could feel her touch or move. At times I wanted to tell her yes because she worried about my sister and I so much and I did not want her to worry about me. But I didn't want to be dishonest because she doesn't deserve that, and it wouldn't be fair to her. It was hard for me to allow my family to see me lying in a hospital bed with a brace around my neck, swollen up and can't move a muscle. They had always seen me as a healthy and strong individual, now I felt like I had let them down and I was embarrassed for them seeing me in this condition. I was unsure what they thought about me. I didn't know if they would be embarrassed to accept me as one of their family members or if they will be accepting of me as they always were. All kinds of thoughts were running through my head. I didn't know what was accurate or inaccurate. It was difficult for me to think positive in this new-found body and mind set. This wasn't a disease that had gradually gotten worse where I would've been able to slowly adjust to circumstances and situations; no this happened within a blink of an eye! One second I was able to function and perform tasks that were essential to everyday living, and the next second I was totally dependent upon nurses, doctors, caregivers and family members doing everything for me.

I found it difficult to adapt to people performing tasks for me that I used to perform for myself and others. For years I've cared for people that was unable to care for themselves. Now the roles were reversed, and I didn't like it but I had to accept it. So now I had two options: to feel sorry for myself and go into a deep depression, or fight like I had never had to fight before. I chose to fight and attempt to regain everything I had lost.

I was accustomed to wearing nice apparel and keeping myself well groomed. Now, caregivers were picking out my clothes every day for me, which consisted of sweats and a T-shirt; appropriate for therapy. I temporarily lost control of my bowel and bladder functions and as a result I had to wear undergarments. I was also catheterized to control my bladder in-take. I had men giving me a shower and dressing me. I was embarrassed and felt less than a man. I didn't like this helplessness at all! But God has a way of humbling all of us. This was a wake-up call for me. I should have been thankful for the help of others, but all I could think about was my self-pride.

I wanted to know more about my injury, so Dr. Ho provided me with more details. My spinal cord was pinched by the vertebrae that had broken my neck. He went on to say that I was blessed because my spinal cord was not severed. If that had been the case the chances of me walking again would have been slim to none, but because mine was only pinched, it was only swollen. Once the swelling subsided, I would regain some of my motor skills. My doctor said that he had seen many patients that had been in a car wreck similar to mine and they did not survive or they had much more of a traumatic injury than mine. I had no broken bones or internal injuries. I had only broken my neck which was a very severe injury in itself. My spinal cord was interrupted at level C3-C6.

I was so thankful that my doctor was a Christian. We both believed in the power of God. He would always tell me that "anything is possible with God. We have to do the possible and let him do the impossible, which meant lots of rehabilitation and a good diet". A few people have asked me "what is it like to have a spinal cord injury?" It is difficult to explain in detail, but the best way I can explain it is this: Imagine some of your muscles not working but other ones does. My legs always feel heavy and stiff, as if I'm trying to walk with a 4yr. old sitting on my feet.

I never questioned God as to why he allowed this to happen to me. I never got upset. I chose to fight with all I had. I knew God would never give me more than I can handle. Remember, when we're put in difficult situations, we have to know that God allowed those things to happen to build our faith and make us stronger. My mom used to say "whatever don't kill you will make you stronger". All of us have people watching our every move, and if they see us fail that gives them the excuse to fail too, but if we make through, it that gives them a reason to make it as well.

Rehab started daily about 8am. I would awake and the caregivers would feed me breakfast and give me a shower every other day. I had to be lifted out of bed with a Hoyer lift, placed in a wheelchair and pushed downstairs to the gym. Because of the severity of my injury, the medical staff wanted to rule out a brain injury, so I was ordered to attend speech therapy classes which consisted of me answering a series of simple to difficult questions. I understand that these tests were necessary, but some of these questions a toddler could answer. After days of these tests, a brain injury was ruled out.

There was a gym full of patients with all kinds of disabilities. Some were in wheelchairs, some were in motorized wheelchairs, some were on crutches, some were on canes and some were walking with walkers. I remember thinking, this is what I have to go through and see every day. It took me a few minutes to take it all in and observe my surroundings. It was almost like a foreign world. I had seen rooms and gyms like this before, but I had walked in and out of them by my own will. I had never sat in a wheelchair before and I never thought that I would ever see it from this perspective.

I wasn't able to do much in the gym but look around and observe some of the exercises that I would soon hope to do. I attended occupational therapy because I was unable to use my hands for fine motor skills. Because my injury was in my cervical, everything below that area of injury was affected. The occupational therapist worked with me to strengthen and regained the activity of my fingers, hands and arms. But while I was in the gym, I did receive electronic stimulation. That was a device where the therapist (Tracy one of many therapists) would put electrodes on my legs and arms, turn the device on to a setting that would make the muscles contract in an attempt to strengthen them. It was very uncomfortable until I got used to it. It felt like shocking and tingling simultaneously. But I could feel my muscles in my arms and legs contract and my fingers would open and close, all of which I was unable to do on my own. After doing that treatment several times a day, my body began to get stronger to where I was able to do exercises in the gym.

Tracy was assisting me transfer from my wheelchair onto a mat table. It was very difficult and exhausting for me to sit upright without falling over. The table felt like I was sitting on a big ball. I had no balance to sit upright, but before I fell over she would catch me. That's when I realized I had a long road ahead of me, but I continued to work hard and strengthen my body and most of all my spirit.

As the days went on, I was able to do more and my body was getting stronger, which meant the swelling was subsiding on my spinal cord. All of the therapists were really nice, friendly and very knowledgeable. I made some friends there and I'm really grateful for all that they did for me.

Ron Wise

CHAPTER 3
IT'S A FAMILY AFFAIR

Support from my family was crucial in my recovery, both physically and mentally. One of my favorite cousins, Sarah Ann, would visit me from Gary, Indiana quite frequently. She always had a smile on her face, full of laughter and very joyful. I always enjoyed seeing her, because she was uplifting and she knew how to make me laugh. We would talk and reminisce about the past and all the fun we used to have. She knew how to take my mind off the current situation and she was truly a blessing to have around.

While I was an inpatient, I also learned that I had a cousin that worked in a hospital close by. I had never met him before. He came to visit and was very friendly and encouraging. He would stop by to visit occasionally and we would sit and talk about family, sports and God. He is a huge University of Michigan football fan and retired military. He told me there was going to be a family reunion held in Grand Rapids, Michigan and he wished that I could make it. I told him I would love to come, but would be unable because I was an inpatient here in the hospital. So, he said I will bring them here to the hospital with disbelief, I said okay".

Within the next few days, the entire lobby was filled with the Wise family I had never met before in my life. I was overwhelmed! But they were very nice and friendly. I felt honored that they all came to the hospital to see a family member they had not met before. It wasn't a coincidence that all of this occurred. I would not have been able to meet this part of my family if I had never had that car wreck. I thank God for making that divine connection through me. Even if we don't understand, God does everything purposeful. God doesn't make mistakes or accidents. That's why I don't call my injury a car accident; it was very purposeful.

My mom traveled back and forth from Chicago to Michigan every weekend to see me and spend time with the kids, my wife and my mother-in-law. My mom has always been there for me when I needed her. My sister and my brother-in-law flew in from Georgia to visit me and provided moral support and comfort. They too are a wonderful couple and I'm so grateful for the time they spent with me. My mother-in-law dropped her life in Las Vegas and moved to Michigan to stand in the gap and help out with anything that was needed. My mother-in-law is a blessing to my entire family. She truly is a second mother to me. My youngest son and daughter were there on the weekends to show support as they saw what therapy looked like for me and witnessed what now became my everyday life. Needless to say, my wife was there with me several days throughout the week, traveling on a snowy and icy road 45 minutes each way. She would get off work and visit with me well into the night hours. I would tell her not to visit on the days she worked, but she would come anyway. I was concerned about her driving on dangerous icy roads, being up all day and being fatigued while driving to see me. I thank God for granting her traveling grace for all those nights. She would literally risk her life just to see her husband. I can honestly say she took her wedding vows very seriously. There are no words to express how much I love her for being the woman that she is.

I have a new appreciation for life. I do not take it for granted and I cherish every moment of it. Everyday our bodies have a way of telling us that we're not going to be here forever, and since the enemy attempted to take me out, I have to testify on his failed attempt on my life. We have to be careful that the enemy does not steal our joy, because our joy is our strength. I thank God for my family. I would not be able to be physically or mentally strong without them. Because my mom was there every weekend, she got a chance to bond more with my kids, wife and mother-in-law. As a result, they all became closer. Once again, it was because of me and my car wreck!!

Throughout the days and weeks, I continued to get stronger. My bladder was functioning more efficiently and the undergarments were discontinued as well. Dr. Ho told me if I continued to make improvements, I would be able to go home for a few hours on the weekend.

Ron Wise

CHAPTER 4
THERE'S NO PLACE LIKE HOME VISITS

It was close to Thanksgiving and I desperately wanted to go home for a few hours to enjoy dinner and spend time with the family. I had worked so hard all month to strengthen my body, but I was unable to make it home. Dr. Ho was not confident that I was strong enough to be out of professional caregiver's care, as I was a huge liability to the hospital. This was truly disappointing for me to hear. Although my hopes were defeated, what happened next was heart-warming. My wife had cooked dinner and she and the kids came to share Thanksgiving dinner with me. The whole family was sitting in one of the common areas watching a football game while she fed me. They stayed for a few hours and then went home. It was sad to see them leave, but I understood. I always wanted her to leave before it got too dark because I was worried about the roads, weather and deer running out of a field in the middle of the road.

I was really happy and excited when Shana visited me but I often felt sad when she left. My mood went from laughing, joking and having a good time, to quiet, sadness and loneliness. I would call her on cell phone and talk to her all the way home just to make sure she didn't fall asleep at the wheel or anything terrible happen to her.

I was determined to get home for a few hours on the weekend, so I continued to push myself to increase my endurance, stamina, and strength. I continued to work hard in the gym and use my last rejected home visit as motivation. I started to see my arms and legs range of motion increase and I felt so proud of myself for having worked so hard and now I was seeing the results of my

29

dedication. I was still unable to stand at this time, but I was overjoyed with just being able to scratch my head and move my legs. It had been a long time since I was able to do anything for myself and now I was seeing my legs move. I even attempted to feed myself. Most of my food fell on my chest and lap, but that was okay because I was trying and I knew as long as I tried it I would get better over time.

A week before Christmas I saw Dr. Ho and we were engaged in a conversation about going home for Christmas. He had been getting reports from the therapist and they were all good. He also said that if I continued improving, he saw no problem with me going home for a few hours on Christmas Day. I was so excited! For years I was a caregiver at the mental hospital in our town. I had taken care of patients that were hospitalized for weeks, months and even years. They would talk about the things they used to do when they were home with their family and loved ones and how they wanted to be discharged and start their lives where they left off. But I never really understood the way they felt until now. I was so excited to know that I will be able to go home just for a few hours and get out of that hospital environment.

On Christmas Eve, I was unable to sleep all night. I was awoke thinking about what my day was going to be like; the food I was going to eat and spending time with my family. I felt just like a kid on Christmas Eve, very anxious and excited. Christmas Day finally arrived and the caregivers assisted me with dressing and grooming. I got into my motorized wheelchair and headed down to the awaiting transporting van. This was my first time having to ride in the back of one of these vans. It had a lift-gate which loaded me and my chair inside the van. They strapped the chair down for safety and I was on my way home.

It felt so good to be out of the hospital and out in the fresh air. Everything looked so different outside. I felt like

I had been locked up and I didn't like it. As the van drove down the street and onto the highway entrance ramp, I would look from left to right, in an attempt to take it all in. I cannot believe how different things looked after only a couple of months. Nevertheless, I was on my way home to see my family and that's what was most important to me.

When I arrived at the house, everyone was excited to see me. The first thing I noticed was my newly installed handicap ramp. The house was decorated festively and everything was perfect. We watched TV, open presents, ate dinner and played games. We were all enjoying each other until it was time for me to leave. I had to return to the hospital by 9 p.m. I felt like Cinderella who was at the ball having a good time but had to be home by midnight. I felt bad about leaving, but I knew I had to. My wife was crying and didn't want me to leave. It was a very sad moment for the both of us. It was difficult for me to leave my home when everyone wanted me to stay and be a family like we had always been. It was a long ride back to the hospital. I thought about how much fun I had and how lonely I was going to be for the remainder of the night. Although I just experienced one of the best days of the past few months, I started to feel a little depressed, so I had to find ways to uplift my spirit. I thought about all the progress I made and how I was continually improving. I knew there would not be many days like this ahead of me as long as I continued to work hard and concentrate on my ultimate goal, which was to be discharged from the hospital.

When I returned to the hospital, I got into bed and thought about my day and was anticipating the next home visit. Even more so, I now longed for the time when I would be discharged. I was motivated more than ever to get stronger and return home to my family permanently. I thought about how the Lord had given me mercy and saved my life from the car wreck. That was when I realized my life had purpose and he had saved my life for a reason.

God is always speaking to us even while we're being disobedient, but all of our lives have purpose and He will only allow disobedience for an allotted amount of time, because his will shall be done. And sometimes he has to put us in a place where we're not distracted and we can hear him speak clearly. In my case it had to be in a hospital room by myself for several lonely nights that ultimately equated to five months before he fully got my attention. When I think about how good God is and how he has saved and transformed my life, I can't help but to praise him.

From that point, I was able to visit home every weekend for a few hours a day. I was steadily gaining mobility and I felt better than I had felt in a long time. I was being more self- sufficient now. I was able to brush my teeth and the nursing staff also disconnected the sip and puff from my handrail of the bed. My legs felt stronger and the therapists were discussing having me stand in the next therapy session. I had not stood upright in months, so I was nervous and a little reluctant because I did not want to fall and have a huge setback. When the day came for me to stand, the therapist laid me on a tilting table that started out flat but stood upright with the therapist controlling the vertical degrees. It would start out flat then tilt up to a 90° angle, but I was unable to achieve the 90° because I would get dizzy. Tracy said I would get dizzy because my body was not used to standing up in a 90° angle, but the more I did it the more my body adjusted to it.

After several sessions, I was proud of the progress that I had been making. I was able to handle being in an upright position without getting dizzy. It also felt good to see things while I was standing in a 90° angle.

I continued making progress with therapy and the therapists continued to challenge my muscles with different activities and to make them stronger, including aquatic therapy. I had never liked the pool, but my therapists encouraged me to try it, so I did. This therapy consisted of standing, weight shifting, in place marching and various other strengthening exercises. These exercises were easier for me because the water took away a lot of the weight of my legs and allowed them to float.

As a kid I never liked the swimming pool because it was uncomfortable for the chlorine water to get in my nose, ears and mouth I was always afraid of drowning. So now that I was in the pool with a spinal cord injury, I felt very vulnerable and unsure of my safety. Even though I had three therapists in the pool with me, and I was totally safe, I still insisted on having floats around my waist and wrists. I felt kind of silly because I was the biggest person in the pool yet I was the most fearful. Nevertheless, I had to push past my fears to do what was best for me. Although it wasn't easy, I had to put my trust in the therapists and know they had my best interest in mind. Needless to say, it was not easy for them to earn my trust, but after several visits to the pool, it became easier for us to work with each other. After several weeks of these exercises, I was able to walk in the pool from one side to the other and my progression was very promising.

Like always, the therapists continued to challenge my muscles and ability. But this time they took it a little bit further. They asked me how I felt about attempting to walk around the gym using a walker. I was very nervous and excited all at that same time. But of course, I welcomed their challenge. Using the walker, I had to stand straight up and lean on it with my forearms for stability. A therapist was on the left and right side of my body. They sat on very low stools with wheels, (like the ones you would see in a doctor's office) and they would help me pick my legs up and advanced them forward

I was unable to do it with my own strength. Although they were helping me advance my legs, this was very exhausting. I had not walked for a while but it felt good to be able to stand upright and see everything from that position. I felt very motivated to continue challenging and pushing myself to my maximum ability.

The home visits became more frequent and the more I visited, the more I wanted to stay. I wanted to sleep in my own bed overnight and enjoy my home life with my family.

I continued to motivate myself any way that I could. I would see patients in the gym struggling with exercises and immobility. After seeing them day after day, week after week and month after month, I was determined to push myself whenever I was in the gym. Granted, I didn't know their limitations or situations, but I did know what mine were and what I needed to do to get better. I'm not saying that I'm any better than them, however you find your motivation to be a better individual, you need to execute it without being disrespectful or boastful. There were patients functioning at a higher rate and that motivated me. Likewise, there were patients that saw my progress and were motivated by my tenacity.

This rehabilitation hospital had patients from all walks of life, careers and professions. The injuries were as varied as the patients. Some had broken arms, some had sustained a brain injury and other had life-long deficits in their bodies. It was like a huge melting pot of patients who were all trying to better themselves to afford them a better quality of life.

My therapists and doctors were so proud of the strength and mobility I had regained, as I continued getting stronger and more self-sufficient. I had regained control of my bladder functioning and did not have to be catharized anymore. This was very exciting news for me and I felt good about my future. I had more mobility in my legs. The right-side of my body was stronger than my left, as I had sustained more nerve damage on the left-side. I started thinking about being more independent and driving. I was pretty confident and motivated to operate a vehicle. I continued to work hard in the gym for the next few weeks. Then one day I built up the nerve to ask Tracy if I could be considered for drivers' training. She said sure and would talk to the other therapists and doctor about it. While in a meeting with them, they gave me some exciting news. They were discussing having me attend driver's education. This was so exciting because that meant I was going to regain my independence back.

When the day arrived for my first class, I was nervous as a teenager taking driver's education for the first time. The classes consisted of a written, vision and a road test which I had to pass to get my license.

All kinds of thoughts were going through my head. I was thinking and concerned about passing or failing the test. I had spoken to Tracy earlier about what the test consisted of. We talked about the difficulty of it and how other patients did. She re-assured me and said she had no doubts that I would not only pass the test with flying colors, but I would exceed the recommended score. Well, I thought the same thing. I just needed someone else to reaffirm my thoughts. The night before my test, I was very nervous and anxious. I had to pass a written and a vision test before I could take the simulated road test. If I failed the test I would have to wait until it was offered again, besides I didn't want any setbacks.

I waited for a couple of days before I received the results of my test. I was on pins and needles because I had tried so hard and I couldn't stand the thought of having to do it all over again. Finally, the results were in. I passed those two tests with no problems! (Praise God) Now it was time for me to take the simulated road test. I was confident that I remembered how to drive, but wasn't sure of my ability. I took the test on a Friday evening. It consisted of acceleration, traveling distance, breaking in a safe time, steering, signaling, and fast reaction thinking time. After the test concluded, I was confident that I did well and was eager to hear my results. I was told that the results would not be available until the following Monday. I knew it would be a long weekend.

Monday finally arrived and it was time for the moment of truth. I had taken my medication, got a shower, ate breakfast and got dressed. I was very eager to know my test results, but I had to attend therapy which would not end until late morning. That meant it would not be until the afternoon before I found out what my test results were.

It was a little past noon when I learned I had passed my driver's education tests. I felt like I was on the fast track to be independent and regained what the devil had stolen from me. This was the best I have felt in a long time, physically and mentally. But I wasn't out of the woods yet. I still had to take and pass an actual road test. To prepare me for the road test, the rehab hospital allowed me to use their driver education vehicle to practice driving around town. On the way to the vehicle, I was a little scared and I was way more nervous than I appeared to be. I didn't want to make my teacher nervous, so I would crack jokes and make small talk. In fact, he enjoyed it so much, that I think he was just as nervous as I was, and we were doing the same thing to each other in an attempt to make each other feel comfortable.

I entered the vehicle with no problem. The first thing I did was say a short prayer asking for traveling grace and mercy. Then I took a deep breath because I couldn't believe I was behind a steering wheel once again. I was about to embark on the very thing that nearly killed me a few of months prior. There are no words to describe the way I was feeling at this point, but I knew I had to push through it. I could not allow the devil to control my mind and talk me out of my independence. I took another deep breath and told myself," I can do all things through Christ who gives me strength" Phil. 4:13. I fastened my seatbelt, because I remembered I was in such a rush trying to make it to work and forgot to fasten my seatbelt when I was in a car wreck a few of months earlier. Without any adaptive driving equipment, I adjusted the seat and the mirrors, then started the vehicle. I gently placed my foot on the brake and put the car in gear. I let off the brake and pressed the gas pedal and began to exit the parking lot. The traffic was moderate and it was cold outside with a light dusting of snow on the streets. I recall thinking to myself, "what are you doing, you're back at it again "I had to tell Satan to get behind me!!! Everything was going well, and the longer I drove, the more comfortable I was. I was driving for about 45 minutes and my instructor was giving me verbal praise. I felt good about how well I was driving and how comfortable it felt. We returned back to the hospital and my instructor said I did very well and he would schedule another appointment for me to get more practice driving on the road.

My confidence level was through the roof and I felt like I could conquer anything anyone threw at me. After a few more of these appointments, my instructor felt like I was ready for the road test. He scheduled a road test at the Department of Motor Vehicles (DMV) for the following week. Again, the devil was feeding me negative thoughts about what I couldn't do, however, his words meant nothing because with God's strength, I had a good track record with overcoming his setbacks and lies.

When I arrived at the DMV, the instructor was really nice and friendly. She briefed me on the points system that she will be using to grade my driving ability and we went out to drive. I entered the vehicle and said a short prayer, asking God for traveling grace and mercy. Again, without any adaptive equipment, I fastened my seatbelt, adjusted my seat and my mirrors and off I went. I wasn't as nervous as I thought I would be, but I was by no means calm. I realized that this was the real thing and I did not, and was not, going to fail. I had come too far to fail.

The roads were snowy and a little slippery. It seemed like everyone was traveling so much faster than I was, zipping in and out of lanes as if they were on a racetrack. No one was using turn signals and they were traveling well above the speed limit. This caused me to have a little bit of concern, because I was always use to keeping up with the flow of traffic, but I couldn't do that now because I had this lady in the passenger seat with a clipboard and pen writing something every few minutes. When I tried to glance over to see what she was writing, she'd pull the clipboard towards her chest, look from above her eyeglasses and smile at me. I'm not sure if she was writing something that was in reference to my driving or if she was making out a grocery list. Either way, I had to continue to focus on what I was doing and following the rules of the road. I attempted to make small talk with her and tell her some of the old jokes that I had told to the rehab hospital instructor, but she wasn't going for it. She was all about business and I knew it wasn't no "getting on her good side". When we returned to the DMV, she asked me to turn off the vehicle and hand her the keys. When we got to her desk, she had a serious look on her face and asked me how do I think I did? I replied "I think I did well" but it didn't matter what I thought, the only thing that mattered is how she thought I did, and if I had passed. The suspense was killing me!! She looked up at me, then looked down at her paper, then looked at me again above her eye glasses, with another serious look, cracked a smile and said "you passed!!". I felt exhilarated, empowered, accomplished and relieved all at the same time. Then she walked over to me and gave me a big hug and said I passed with flying colors. She went on to congratulate me and wished me well on my road to independence. I had accomplished another milestone within my journey to independence.

FROM TRAGEDY TO TRIUMPH

CHAPTER 5
DISCHARGED: HOMEBOUND

About a month after I got my driver's license, the doctor and the therapists were discussing a topic that I had waited months to discuss - discharging me!! They inquired about the floor plan and lay out of my home in great detail. They wanted to know the whereabouts of the restrooms and if the doors were wide enough for a wheelchair. They inquired about the tub and shower and how safe it was for entering and exiting safely. They also inquired about the stairs that were in the home.

We lived in a house that had 17 stairs to the upper level, all the bedrooms were located, including the master bedroom. I was strong, but not yet strong enough to navigate a flight of stairs safely. I knew this would pose a potential problem. Nevertheless, I continued to stay encouraged and think positive. The therapists arranged a home evaluation. They wanted to see what modifications were needed in order for me to be discharged.

The therapists came to evaluate the house. She took pictures and measured every door frame and room. They were very thorough and detailed. Following the evaluation, she made several recommendations. I would need a stair lift chair to navigate the stairs safely.

I could not be discharged until it was installed and operable. This meant that my discharge would be prolonged. I was very unhappy with this decision, but I understood it was all in my best interest and safety. I would also need a ramp to enter and exit the house. Other recommendations included grab bars to be installed in the showers and by the toilets.

Within a couple of weeks later, the stair lift was installed. The entry and exit ramps were installed the following months. There were no more modifications needed in the house.

Finally, I felt like there could be no more setbacks and delays for my discharge. I was eager and ready to go. I had seen patients be admitted after me and discharged before me. Patients would ask me, "when are you getting discharged?" and some of the nursing staff would tell me they can't recall anyone being an inpatient as long as I had been there. Dr. Ho would tell me that I can leave anytime I get ready, but I had a specific goal in mind. I was admitted to the hospital on a gurney. I had told my wife that I will walk again. I was determined to walk out of the hospital no matter what anyone said or thought about me. I had been hospitalized for five months and the day had come for me to be discharged.

My wife had gathered all of the "get well cards" off the wall and my personal blanket that was on my bed.

I had gotten comfortable seeing my room personalized and now it was starting to look like the room that I had entered on my first day as an inpatient. As I looked around the room, it took me a little while to take it all in, as if my mind was in overdrive. I was definitely ready to leave, but at the same time, I knew that I would miss the staff and all they had done for me.

All of my belongings packed and ready to go. My wife and kids were waiting impatiently for the nurse and the doctor to finish the discharge paperwork and give me my supply of medication. It seemed like

eternity, but now they were finally letting me go. It was a bitter sweet moment to be leaving the people that provided such great nursing care for me. It was almost as if they were my family and I was leaving them. The nursing staff and therapists were all in my room giving me hugs, taking pictures and wishing me well. It was a long walk from my room to the parking lot, so I got in a wheelchair and was wheeled down the hallway. As I passed other patient rooms, they yelled "congratulations", "take care".

When I got downstairs to the exit door, I got out of the

chair and walked about 5 feet to the car. It was a short walk, but nevertheless I came in the hospital paralyzed from the neck down on a gurney. but on March 16, 2011, I walked out of that same hospital. I had made my wife a promise and I was determined to keep it no matter how hard it was. I didn't believe the lies the devil had whispered to me.

I had always taught my kids to never give up and fight when times get hard. Now, I had to live up to the words that I had taught them. This has by far been the hardest test of my life and I was determined to pass it. It was time for me to lead by example. I did not want my kids to see me as a failure and that fueled my motivation to push past my circumstances. I had to show them if I can make it through the toughest time of my life, then they can make it through tough times that they will have to endure. My physical condition was not just about me, but about the life that I lead for my family. I needed to be able to ambulate and use my body the way that I did prior to my injury. At times it was very difficult for me to envision that I would regain 100 percent free movement. I had to be a strong individual no matter how weak my body felt. My goal was to be more self- sufficient and healthier.

It felt good to be home, and especially having to leave the hospital. We had the home care instructions from the nursing staff, but I was still a little nervous. For months I had been under professional nursing care and although my wife is a nurse, my kids and mother-in-law would help me with my daily needs. I was nervous about being home without the professional nursing staff that I was so accustomed to.

Before I was discharged, I was scheduled to continue therapy at the hospital. At the time it had seemed like a great idea for me to continue therapy with therapist whom I was familiar with and they were familiar with me. I commuted back-and-forth which took 45 minutes each way. Shana and I agreed that it was too long of a commute.

After about six weeks, we decided to find a closer rehab facility. I soon started attending a rehab facility that was approximately 7 minutes away from my home. The therapists were really nice and friendly. They were astonished that I had as much mobility as I did and was also able to ambulate as well as I did. They went on to say that I was lucky because most patients that have an injury such as mine did not survive or gain very little or no return. I told them that I was not lucky, but I was blessed by a miracle from God. I was attending occupational therapy and physical therapy for an hour five days a week. It had appeared to me that getting stronger and healthier had become my new full-time job, but this new job was far more difficult than the previous one or any job that I had ever held. My wife would help me with the majority of my daily needs like showering, food preparations, toileting etc., but everybody rallied together to help me out. I felt a little awkward having my kids assist with getting me dressed and undressed. It made me feel less than a man. They had to assist me with the very thing that I assisted them with as kids and now the roles were reversed and that didn't sit too well with me. I would get frustrated because although I had regained some mobility in my hands, I had lost my fine motor skills with my fingers. Without the use of fine motor skills, that made life very difficult for me to achieve what otherwise had been easy tasks like pulling a zipper up or down, tying a shoe, or button a shirt etc.... I felt embarrassed to ask for help. But after a few mishaps, I quickly learned to set aside my pride and ask for the help I most desperately needed.

It was really nice being home, because I was able to go to the mall, go to a friend's house, out to eat, attend church service etc... A lot of people were happy to see me back in church and others didn't know why I was gone for several months. They were asking me how I had injured myself and if I would ever regain all of my mobility. These were some of the same questions that I had asked Dr. Ho

However, they were just being inquisitive and concerned as I was about myself. I was unable to answer all of their questions, so I told them "whatever God has for me, that's what I will get, and I have learned to be satisfied with that".

After consulting my doctor, I was able to slowly discontinue taking some of my medication. I went from taking a handful of medications, to taking two medications. I felt good as I was walking with a walker throughout the house, but I was not satisfied with my progress. I didn't want to walk with any assisted devices. I was happy that I was able to walk, after all that was one of my goals that I had set for myself, but I wanted more strength so that I could have more mobility. But it just wasn't happening fast enough for me but the Bible tells me to be anxious for nothing (Phil.4:6).

I was unsure if I had plateaued or if I would get more mobility in my body later. The only thing I could do was the possible and allow God to do the impossible. Although I am a man of faith, I questioned God about my future and what it held for me. I began to worry about the condition of my body 20, 30 or even 40 years from today. How will I feel? What condition will I be in? I had a lot of questions that needed to be answered by God himself because no one else had the answers. I would pray day in and day out and it seemed like God wasn't hearing me. I didn't understand why he wasn't answering me. I have prayed and asked God questions in the past and he had clearly answered them, but this time was different. My prayers and questions were unanswered.

Then one day, it made sense to me. God doesn't answer all of our questions and prayers, because sometimes we can't handle the truth!!! Oftentimes we want our prayers and questions answered, but if we knew the answers to all of our questions and prayers we would probably do something that we wouldn't otherwise do. I thank God for answering me. So, whether I have plateaued

44

or if I continued to gain mobility, I thank God for his will
(and not mine) being accomplished in my life

CHAPTER 6
TRAVELING AND DEPRESSION

The family would often travel from Kalamazoo to Flint, MI, and to Chicago, and Gary Indiana to visit family members. The travel time was only about 2 hours to each of those destinations. But my body was not used to traveling for that period of time. It took a little getting used to. We would stop every so often to rest and I utilized that time to stretch and loosen up a bit. I soon began to notice that the more frequently we travelled, the more my body adjusted. We would travel quite a bit and I felt pretty good about it. There were so many places I wanted to visit but did not have the opportunity because of my work-load. But now I had the time and I was going to take advantage of it. I talked to my wife and kids about going to Disney World. They were all excited and eager to go. I was a little nervous because I had not traveled that long of a distance in a while. I was unsure of how my body would react to that long of a distance. I had not traveled in an airplane since before my injury. This caused me to be a little concerned. I was concerned about being cramped in the small seating of the airplane for several hours. There would be no lay-over and I would not have the luxury of standing and stretching to loosen my body. What if I had to use the restroom and needed help while I was in there? Or what if I had an accident and had to return to my seat with everyone seeing this huge mess I made on myself. What if I would have to crawl over the passengers I was seated next to in order to return to my seat. I wouldn't want to bring any extra attention to myself, but it would be inevitable. I am 6'5" in statue, so naturally when I stood up on a plane people eyes and attention would be drawn to me. I was still very self-conscience about people overly observing me and the way I walked.

But isn't it funny how the devil can get in your head and tell you lies to keep you from the accomplishing the goals that God has already made provisions for you to succeed in. But (John 8:44) says there is no truth in him and he is the father of lies. This wasn't the first time he whispered lies to me, so I was up for the challenge. It was 10pm when we arrived at the Airport. I was escorted to the departure gate in a wheelchair by one of the airport attendants. They allowed me to board the airplane first. I walked down the aisle and held on to the seats along both sides until I got to my row, then sidestepped into my seat and sat down. Shana asked me how I felt. I said was a little uncomfortable but the truth of the matter is, I was very uncomfortable. I took a few deep breaths and soon settled in. The flight was a couple hours long and I was anticipating arriving in Orlando Florida and quickly exiting the airplane. When the plane landed and came to a complete stop, I stood up and completed a series of much needed stretches. Needless to say, the concerns that I previously had upon boarding were not a concern at all. The combination of sitting for a long period of time, combined with the air conditioning made me stiffer than usual.

Upon exiting, there was an attendant with a wheelchair waiting to wheel me to the gate. From that point, we all got into a golf cart and was driven to baggage claim. When we received our baggage and my walker, exited the airport and hailed a cab to the hotel. The city of Orlando was beautiful, as there were palm trees everywhere, beautiful flowers and nicely manicured lawns. I had been here when I was a kid, but so much had changed since then. When we arrived at the hotel, Shana and I were exhausted, but the kids were still excited and wanted to go to the hotel pool. It had been a long day, so we decided to get a good night sleep and start fresh in the morning.

Although I was exhausted, it had taken me a while to un-wind and wrap my head around what I had just accomplished. Just a few months prior, I was in a hospital bed being spoon-fed and unsure if I would ever be able to feed myself and other daily living activities. And now I had walked on and off an airplane and was several states away from home. I had finally fell asleep and awakened refreshed.

We started our day with a shower and breakfast. We caught the shuttle bus to the parks and rented a scooter for me as we visited several of the theme parks and enjoyed some shopping. Shana and the kids rode the rides. Needless to say, I wanted to ride, but I wasn't that brave. I was not going to chance getting injured on a ride and incur a setback. But then I started to think, I can probably ride a less intensive ride and still be safe, but I quickly came to my senses and dismissed that thought. I really enjoyed us being together and spending family time with one another. It had been so long since we had a family outing together like this one, and I really enjoyed seeing their smiling faces. Shana didn't want to ride all the rides the kids rode and vice versa, so they alternated and hung out with me. We enjoyed Disney for a few days then went home. The flight home was the same as it was flying into Orlando. We had a great time on our vacation, but it was really nice to be home. Since then, we have traveled to Puerto Rico, Jamaica, Bahamas and several cities and states.

Summer had begun and I started to get depressed because I was unable to be active and enjoy the summer like I did in the previous years. I reminisced about our trips to South Haven beach and how we all played in the sand and water. There were many things that I would not be able to do that caused me to be concerned. It was depressing to see everybody around me doing whatever they wanted to do with little or no effort involved. I was not depressed because of their ability; I was depressed because of my inability. I would witness them perform simple tasks that would be impossible for me to duplicate. Simple tasks, like tying a shoe, buttoning a shirt or even simply walking was difficult or impossible for me to do. I knew I had a lot to be thankful for, but my faith was really being tested. The harsh reality of what my life currently was and what it was going to be began to overshadow my future and my faith. I felt like I had no one to talk to that would understand what I was going through or what I was up against. Shana suggested counseling or finding a support group, but I rejected both of those ideas. I felt like I was being held captive in my own body and I just wanted to be free. Even if I did have someone to talk to, it would not had made a difference. I did not want a pep talk or hear how good God had been. I was fed up. I did not want to be healed I wanted to be made whole. The only thing I thought about was I had the rest of my life to live with some type of deficit within my body. As I continued to watch my family go about their life effortlessly around me, I quickly did a visual scan of my body. Although it appears to be without deficits, that was a very misleading and deceptive assumption. I found myself having to ask for help more often than I was comfortable with. I began to see myself as more of a burden to my family. I went from a strong and able person, to someone who was dependent upon my family for simple daily living tasks. They attempted to convince me that they did not have a problem with assisting me, but I could see that it was a little uncomfortable for them as well as it was for me. This was a lifestyle we were not accustomed to and it was not an easy transition. Having a spinal cord injury has taught me a great deal about people and "so-called" friends. Before my injury my "friends" were plentiful, but once I was injured, there few then tapered down to a handful. I feel as though some associate with me out of kindness, not because it is genuine. It really shows when someone isn't genuinely interested in your company and just in your presence because of obligation or happenstance. I understand that people enjoy the company of someone who they feel comfortable around and able to be active and mobile as they are, but that's no reason why one should ignore me when another able-bodied male enters the room. I was treated as though I was not even in the same house, let alone the same room.

Our conversation came to a halt and I became invisible to the host. The hospitality I was shown was disrespectful and uninviting. But I don't hold grudges, I'm quick to forgive and move on. While we were running errands and taking care of business, I found myself staying behind in the car, because at times I didn't feel like walking. My legs always feel heavy and stiff, and as a result; my walking became a struggle and some-what less important. I found reasons not to walk, and when I did walk, it was always a well thought-out shortest and safest route. I not only had to think about the route I was taking, I also had to literally contemplate every step I took, because my gait was so unsteady. The therapists told me if I would regain any functionality, it would occur roughly within 6 to 8 months after my injury date, and I was well past that time-frame now. I know God can make me whole, but what if He doesn't? Will I have to live the remainder of my life struggling with daily living? The strengthening exercises were not deeming any more results, and that made me more frustrated. I realized I fell into a deep depression, but I didn't want any antidepressant medication. I knew I had to snap out of it before the enemy kill me with stress and possible suicide. I never had a plan of suicide, but I can't say it didn't cross my mind. (John 10:10) The enemy comes to kill steal and destroy. I came that you may have life to the fullest. The enemy knows our weaknesses and he will find ways to encourage us to participate in activities that isn't Gods will. When we find ourselves thinking about unrighteous behavior, we need to quickly put those thoughts in-check before they become an action. Many of us enter dangerous territory because we feed our flesh with inappropriate fleshly actions, instead of recognizing it is all a trick of the enemy. Shana began to pray for me and encouraged me to press on. She challenged me to not only think about my life, but the lives that had been impacted because of my testimony. That was enough for me to continue on, because I realized at that moment that I can have a positive or negative impact on my loved-ones. I did not want people to speak negative about my life, so I dug deep within me to fight yet another round with the enemy. The month was November, and the season was starting to transition. It was cold outside and my body was experiencing a significant amount of stiffness due to the cold weather. The cold weather made it very difficult for me to walk. It felt as though my muscles were locked up. My family and I would continue to go on outings, as I would try to endure the cold weather. I never enjoyed the cold weather, but now it had become more difficult since I had sustained my SCI injury. I knew this would be a very difficult winter for me and I also knew I didn't want to spend another winter season in Michigan.

CHAPTER 7
SOUTH OF THE BORDER

My thoughts were relocating to a warmer climate, as my body would adapt better. But before I put my thoughts in action, I had a lot to think about. I had to take my family into consideration. Shana was born and raised here, her job and all of her friends were here, and the kids would have to make new friends and attend school in a state that was foreign to them. We were living in a huge three level home on a hill with a three-car garage and I did not want to leave that behind and start over again. Everything that we had become accustomed to and worked hard to achieve was going to be a thing of the past. I was really worried about presenting my thoughts to my family because I was unsure if they would be upset with what I was contemplating. I knew what I had to do. I had to seek the Lord for guidance and direction. Jer. 33:3 NIV Call to me and I will answer you and tell you great and unsearchable things you do not know. I knew the Lord would answer me if I petitioned him. I began to fast and pray. I asked the Lord to reveal to me how He wanted me to lead my family. I had no idea what state I wanted to reside in, however I was sure it had to be a warm climate most of the year. I was aware of the many options but not one of the states stood out in my mind. After many prayers, the Lord revealed to me in a vivid dream that I was living in Florida and starting a new life. In my dreams, we had bought a big new house with palm trees in front of it and Shana and the kids were happy and enjoying all the amusement parks, fishing, swimming, and many of Florida tourist attractions. I didn't have any dreams of any other state. After a while, I accepted what he was revealing to me and it was obvious we were relocating to Florida. First, I asked Shana what her thoughts were in regards of relocating, and surprisingly she was all for it. She said she understood how it felt and would not be opposed to relocating to a warmer climate year-round. That conversation went better than I thought it would. I spoke to my 2 oldest sons about it, and they were excited about it, as they would have a place to visit and possibly reside if that was their choice. I didn't have to convince them at all, but I wasn't out of the woods yet. I had two more people I had to speak to, and something was telling me that the conversation would be much different. As I gathered my thoughts to speak to the kids, I asked the Lord to give me the words to say and allow them to be understanding as Shana was. I took a deep breath and began to explain to them what our thoughts were and how the weather had a negative impact on my body. As I began to speak to them, they explained to us how they didn't want to relocate and start their life over again. Imani and Justin best friends lived here and they didn't want to depart from them. They had plans to attend the same high school and college together, and if we relocated, all those dreams would be disrupted. I assumed they would initially be selfish with their thoughts and it would take more convincing than expected. I explained to them that family is more important than friends and they could come back to Michigan and their friends could visit us in Florida. After we reassured their well-being, they were convinced that relocating would be the best option for us as a family. Now we had to decide what city we were going to reside in. We didn't want to be on the coast of the Atlantic Ocean because of hurricanes flooding and damage to our home, so south Florida was not an option. My sister and brother-in-law lives in Georgia and I have family in Alabama, so it made sense to live close to them so we could visit them more frequently. So, we decided to relocate to Jacksonville, Florida.

We were excited and nervous all at the same time. We were searching for homes to rent in Florida via Internet.

We had a lot of work to do before we left Michigan. We were going to have a garage sale to sell some of the items we were not going to bring with us, retrieve boxes to put our household items in, contact a moving company etc... It was all surreal and a little intimidating, as we were about to relocate to an unknown area where we had no family or friends. I was really trusting God with this decision that I had made. But I would be lying if I said I was not a little nervous. I had made a big decision when it pertain to my family and myself before but this one was different. This was one of the biggest decisions I ever had to make. This decision did not just pertain to me moving the family a few miles away, it was much larger than that. What if the kids did not like it, or Shana regretted it. My mother-in-law was relocating to Florida as well as she had lived in various cities around the country. But what if she had said that Jacksonville was the worst city she's ever lived in. I felt as though there was a lot of pressure on me for everyone.

Suddenly I felt a big lump in my throat and questioned this move. But I had to quickly put those thoughts under submission. Exodus 23:20 See, I am sending a angel ahead of you to guard you along the way and to bring you to a place I have prepared. If we're not careful the enemy will attempt to talk us out of what the Lord has already ordained for us. The Lord will allow the enemy to tempt us because he wants to know how faithful we are to him. But I am living proof that there are blessings through your obedience.

After searching several houses for rent, my wife and I flew to Jacksonville to decide on which house we were going to rent. Once we decided, everything moved pretty quickly. When we returned home, we had a garage sale and contacted a moving company. We visited all of our friends and family the last few days we were in town. They all were sad about us leaving, but everyone understood that we were starting a new chapter in our lives. It was a very joyous and sad occasion, but we were all looking forward to what the future held for us.

Once we arrived in Jacksonville, it was foreign territory to us as we did not know anyone or the area we lived in. It did not take us long to unpack and get the house together because we worked on it daily until it was complete. My mother-in-law (Liz), rented an apartment that was nearby and was getting accustomed to the city. Everyone expressed how much we all enjoyed Jacksonville and had high hopes for the future. Wow, it was such a relief to know that everybody was happy and content with the move. We drove all around in an attempt to learn the city and it was fun learning the area, stores, and streets. It was a lot different from Kalamazoo. It was much larger with more activities and fun things to do. It was refreshing to see all the palm trees, tropical plants and totally different scenery. Once we were able to navigate our surroundings and living environments, it was time to make some fun memories in our new state.

We as a family maintained a good social life. We often went bowling. When I was physically able to bowl my bowling average was about 120, which wasn't that great, but it was good enough to beat my family. Although I don't bowl anymore, I enjoy watching my family bowl and compete against one another. It's still fun to see them having a great time. I feel more like a coach on the sideline giving pointers and critiquing their bowling experiences. We try to have fun and enjoy each other as much as possible, because we realize that tomorrow isn't promised and each day we're living on Grace that has been extended from God.

CHAPTER 8
WATER LOGGED

Once I got settled in our home, I researched a physiatrist to treat me for my spinal cord injury. I discovered Dr. Kenneth Ngo (No) of Brooks Rehabilitation in Jacksonville Fl; a well-known, highly knowledgeable and respected Dr. that cares for his patients with great care. His team of staff members are professional and kind. Since I've been injured, I've had the opportunity to study and learn more about my injury. As a result, I run different ideas to him about different information I've discovered. He listens to all my ideas, in regards of my health, well-being and safety. No matter how outlandish my ideas may sound, he listens and gives me his expert opinion and advice, and I totally trust him with my care.

Over the years we have developed a mutual respect for one another and he is one of the best doctors I've had the pleasure to be treated by. He genuinely cares for his patients and does not "push pills" for financial gains. He's a man of great integrity and treats me with dignity and respect. I am blessed to be under his care and staff.

Jacksonville is known for its many bridges. And where there are bridges, there is plenty of water. Everywhere you go, you will see a body of water. While I am not a big fan of the water, my family can't get enough of it. We'd often spend the weekend at the beach. We would grill, the kids and Shana would swim in the ocean, and me and my mother-in-law would watch all the festivities from our comfortable and safe beach chairs. Sometimes we would visit our neighborhood swimming pool. I did like exercising in the warm pool as it would relax my leg muscles.

My family also enjoyed fishing. I myself was never a fisherman or even enjoyed fishing. It was always boring and uneventful for me. But watching my family test their reeling skills, provided me with lots of entertainment and laughter. Shana has her unique style of fishing. She won't bait or take the fish off the hook. My daughter (Imani) loves to fish with the pole in one hand and her phone in the other. When my son (Justin) catches a fish, he is afraid to take the hook out of the fish mouth. My mother-in-law (Liz) enjoys feeding the fish fresh worms and shrimp! She tries so hard to catch a fish, but ultimately the fish really appreciate her hard work and efforts as they take her bait. My brother-in-law (B.J) brags about being the only fisherman, but early mornings and late nights with no catches proves that his best fishing is done at the local supermarket at the seafood counter. My little 7-year-old niece Nae Nae, caught a little fish with a Barbie themed kids fishing pole. Once the fish was off the hook, we gave it to her and she released it back into the water. We all were excited about her catch. She said she was the best fisher girl, and I must agree!

One of my fondest and funniest memories happened when we all had the opportunity to rent and ride jet-skis. None of us were experienced at riding these water crafts, but we thought it would be a fun experience. They all enjoy water-themed activities. And although I don't care for being in a large body of water unless I'm on a boat, I decided to overcome my fears and enjoy this opportunity. We all put on our safety vests and mounted the jet-ski. The kids shared one and Shana and I shared the other one. We received the rules and guidelines and off we went.

The kids quickly fell off the ski. With no injuries, they easily mounted up and continued riding. It was fun and exhilarating to ride in the open water. But the fun didn't last too long. Shana was operating the jet-ski and made a bad turn, and we both fell in the water. We were not hurt, but I was sub-merged under water momentarily and I immediately started to panic. Water entered my ears, nose and mouth and all I could think about was what may have been lurking in the depths of the water and me being unable to swim. We were in a huge river with God-knows what creatures in it. I felt something hit my leg under water and I was not sure if it was Shana or something else. My mind was telling me it was a unknown creature in the water, but I wasn't positive. Nevertheless, I wanted out of the water immediately. The jet-ski started to float away from us and I was getting more worried. I was kicking, screaming and half-way crying. I lost all my dignity as a man and was depending on Shana to save my life. She was struggling and I could see it all over her face, and that brought a great sense of concern. I felt vulnerable and helpless, I was unable to come to my wife's rescue when she needed help and I felt really bad about that.

I gathered my thoughts and tried to calm myself down so that she could concentrate on rescuing both of us. I took a few deep breaths and smiled at her and said "ok we can do this". We tried to tread water towards the jet-ski, but it continued to float away from us. We were only in the water for about 10 minutes, but it felt like eternity. We saw other boaters and jet-ski riders in the distance and they saw us waving for help, but they thought we were waving to say hello, so they waved back, they didn't know we needed help, and the motors on their water-crafts were too loud to hear us yell for help.

Of course, the kids were nowhere to be found, so we were left to fend for ourselves. In an attempt to keep my mind from racing and to keep her calm, I stopped kicking and panicking. I laid on my back and looked up at the sky and a sense of peace overtook me. She became calm and grabbed me by the arms and began to pull me towards the jet-ski.

We got closer and closer to the jet-ski and finally we we're able to pull it towards us. But I was unable to mount it. She struggled trying to assist me in mounting it, but was unsuccessful in all her efforts.

We were so close to being out of the water. It seemed like all our efforts were in vain, and we both were very exhausted and worried. What started out as a good idea, was suddenly turning into a terrible situation. But I couldn't turn back now. I had to get us out of the situation. The water was cool, so my body was tensing up, which made it difficult to move my arms and legs.

Shana was an experienced swimmer, but her rescue skills were poor to nonexistent. Her brother B.J arrived on his jet ski. He jumped into the water to help Shana. B.J was a life saver! Without hesitation he sprang into action, as if he saves lives for an occupation. Both of them were on each side of me helping me to get back on the jet ski. That was not an easy task, as they had to lift my heavy legs and body. But I managed to muster up all my strength and got back on the jet ski, because I was ready to get back to the dock A.S.A.P!!!

When we get back to the dock, we all laughed and joked about the incident. In hindsight it was funny, but it wasn't anything funny about it during that moment. From time- to-time we reminisce about this very day and laugh all over again as if it was yesterday. Overall, it was really a fun and exciting experience. I would do it all over again, but I would be much more careful the next time.

On a different day we had the opportunity to enjoy another outing on the water, one that was safer for me. Florida has many bodies of water, and although I'm not a huge fan of being in the water, I do enjoy being on the water. It brings a calming sense of peace and relaxation. I wasn't in a rush to get back into the water, but I did want to cruise up and down the St. Johns River. We rented boat and cruised up and down the river. I sat in the seat closest to the center of the boat with my life preserver on. I was not taking any chances of me being a man over board with no life preserver on. I'm sure I looked silly, but I rather look silly and be safe. While on the boat, we drunk iced tea, lemonade, played dominoes, cards, listened to music and reminisced about our eventful evening. The kids swam and jumped off the boat into the water, and was pulled behind the boat in a tube. They asked if I wanted to join them, although it looked fun and I cheered them on I kindly declined, I had enough of being in the water for a while! The sun was going down and we had the opportunity to enjoy the sunset.

Beautiful memories like these will never be forgotten, and I'm happy to be a part of them. I'm forever grateful to have a fun-loving family to share these experiences with.

CHAPTER 9
KINGDOM BUILDING: A WISE CHOICE

There is over 700 Churches in the Jacksonville and surrounding area, so we had an abundance of churches to choose from. Shana decided to go on Craigslist to seek a church to attend. She found Christian Leaders Fellowship Church, where Bishop Izell Kirkpatrick is the pastor. First lady Dr. Pamela Kirkpatrick and the entire congregation were very hospitable and welcoming. We visited their church several times and shortly decided we were going to join their church and make it our home. It was a smaller Church than what we were accustomed to, but it was very warm and inviting. Everyone was friendly and happy to have us.

Bishop Kirkpatrick (Bishop K) sermons and teachings were interesting and thought provoking, which opened our minds to another level of spiritual awareness. We felt as though we could grow more spirituality in this church. We were eager to share our gifts and begin serving. We participated in various Ministries and attended many training classes. Bishop K had seen our hard work, dedication and growth throughout our few months of serving, and asked how we felt about being ordained in January of 2013. We accepted the titles with humility and a great sense of gratitude. The first Sunday of January had come and we were scheduled to be ordained as Minister Shana Wise and Deacon Ron Wise. We were both excited and overjoyed with the responsibility of doing God's work and helping to grow his kingdom.

We continue to learn and study under Bishop K teachings and Leadership. We all have a God given gift, many of us have several gifts. One of Shana gifts is to preach the gospel. Bishop K recognized that and suggested that she

be ordained as an Elder. In January 2014 Shana was
ordained as Elder Wise. We worked hand-in-hand with
Bishop K and his ministry. We taught Sunday school,
Bible study and sat on panels for open discussions.
God continued call us to a higher level of Ministry. In
January 2016 Shana was ordained as a Pastor and we
started a bible study group known as Food, Facts and
Fellowship online and in our home. After 6 months of the
bible study group we launched our very own church
known as Wise Choice Ministries. God continues to
motivate us to seek and save the lost. We understand that
there is a calling on our life to spread the gospel, and as a
result, lives are being saved and changed by our obedience
to God. If I can inspire and encourage someone to live in
a positive and Godly manner, then my God is well pleased
with me.

As of today, there is no known cure for a spinal cord
injury, and it is said to be a lifelong condition. I continue
to exercise regularly and maintain a healthy diet, and I have
faith that God can not only heal me but He is able to make
me whole, if it's His will. I am very blessed and thankful to
share my journey and testimony with you. It Has been a
life altering experience, and I'm thankful that He spared
my life to testify on how good He is. I pray that this book
has blessed you and encouraged you to push past your
carnal state of mind and tap into your spiritual mind. I
know that God is able to do exceedingly abundantly above
all that we ask or think, according to the power that works
in us. (Eph. 3:20.) I give God all the glory and all the
honor.

FROM TRAGEDY TO TRIUMPH

FINAL REMARKS AND DEDICATION

I dedicate this book to my beloved father Mr. Randy M. Wise.

My dad along with my mom Mrs. Kitty Wise has been very influential in my life and who helped mold me to who I am as a person today. I praise God for them, and the life they provided for me as a child.

I first want to thank God for preserving my life and allowing me to write this book. I give him all the honor and glory. I pray it be encouraging and a blessing to the reader.

Special thanks to my wife Shana, for loving, encouraging and believing in me. My sister Wendy Brooks, my kids Chris, DeVon, Imani and Justin, my Mother-in-law Liz Hennings, my brother-in-law's, Harris Brooks and William Hennings. Thanks for all your support and love.

Thanks to Pastor Moore and First Lady Gwendolyn Moore of Mt. Zion Baptist Church in Kalamazoo MI. Thanks to all the members and clergy who visited me, prayed and stood in the gap while I was being treated in I.C.U. The prayers and support really meant a lot to me. Thank you, Dr. Joshua Ellwitz of Bronson Methodist Hospital, who performed my surgery.

Thank you to all Bronson medical staff, and Mary Freebed Rehabilitation Hospital staff, Dr. Sam Ho, O.T, P.T, Nurses, Nurse Aids, and everyone who cared for me with "top of the line" care during my 5 months of inpatient.

Thanks to Bishop Kirkpatrick and First Lady Pam Kirkpatrick now of Empowerment Church of Jacksonville Fl, and all the members for being our friends and encouraging me to write this book.

God bless you all,
Ron

Ron Wise

ABOUT THE AUTHOR

Ron is the CFO of Wise Choice Ministries Inc., which he founded with his wife Shana in 2016. He was ordained as a Deacon in 2014 under Bishop Izell Kirkpatrick. Ron worked in the medical field 10 years for the State of Michigan until 2011 when he sustained a spinal cord injury which left him disabled. He is married with four children, Chris, DeVon, Imani, and Justin.

Made in the USA
Columbia, SC
09 March 2023